U.S. Department
of Transportation

**Federal Aviation
Administration**

**FAA-S-8081-22
with Change 1**

I0159562

PRIVATE PILOT

Practical Test Standards

for

GLIDER

APRIL 1999

**FLIGHT STANDARDS SERVICE
Washington, DC 20591**

PRIVATE PILOT

Practical Test Standards

for

GLIDER

1999

FLIGHT STANDARDS SERVICE
Washington, DC 20591

NOTE

Material in FAA-S-8081-22 will be effective April 1, 1999. All previous editions of the Private Pilot—Glider Practical Test Standards will be obsolete as of this date.

RECORD OF CHANGES

Change 1—9/1/2010

IV. AREA OF OPERATION: LAUNCHES AND LANDINGS

G. TASK: Aerotow – Abnormal Occurrences
Q. TASK: Landings – Normal and Crosswind Landing

- To clarify the intent, extent, and condition of the evaluation.

FOREWORD

The Private Pilot—Glider Practical Test Standards (PTS) book has been published by the Federal Aviation Administration (FAA) to establish the standards for private pilot certification practical tests for the glider category. FAA inspectors and designated pilot examiners shall conduct practical tests in compliance with these standards. Flight instructors and applicants should find these standards helpful during training and when preparing for practical tests.

L. Nicholas Lacey
Director, Flight Standards Service

CONTENTS

INTRODUCTION

General Information

The Flight Standards Service of the Federal Aviation Administration (FAA) has developed this practical test book as a standard to be used by FAA inspectors and designated pilot examiners when conducting private pilot—glider practical tests. Flight instructors are expected to use this book when preparing applicants for practical tests. Applicants should be familiar with this book and refer to these standards during their training.

Information considered directive in nature is described in this practical test book in terms, such as "shall" and "must" indicating the actions are mandatory. Guidance information is described in terms, such as "should" and "may" indicating the actions are desirable or permissive, but not mandatory.

The FAA gratefully acknowledges the valuable assistance provided by many individuals and organizations throughout the aviation community who contributed their time and talent in assisting with the revision of these practical test standards.

These practical test standards may be accessed through the Internet at www.fedworld.gov/pub/faa-att/faa-att.htm, or by modem at 703-321-3339. You may purchase these standards from the Superintendent of Documents, U.S. Government Printing Office, Washington, DC 20402.

Changes to these standards, in accordance with AC 60-27, Announcement of Availability: Changes to Practical Test Standards, will be available through the Internet and then later incorporated into a printed revision. For a listing of changes, AFS-600's Internet web site may be accessed at www.mmac.jccbi.gov/afs/afs600.htm.

Comments regarding this publication should be sent to:

U.S. Department of Transportation
Federal Aviation Administration
Flight Standards Service
Airman Testing Standards Branch, AFS-630
P.O. Box 25082
Oklahoma City, OK 73125

Practical Test Standard Concept

Title 14 of the Code of Federal Regulations (14 CFR) part 61 specifies the areas in which knowledge and skill must be demonstrated by the applicant before the issuance of a private pilot certificate or rating. The CFR's provide the flexibility to permit the FAA to publish practical test standards containing the AREAS OF OPERATION and specific TASKS in which pilot competency shall be demonstrated. The FAA shall revise this book whenever it is determined that changes are needed in the interest of safety. Adherence to the provisions of the regulations and the practical test standards is mandatory for the evaluation of private pilot applicants.

Test Book Description

This test book contains the practical test standards for private pilot—glider. This includes the AREAS OF OPERATION and TASKS required for the issuance of an initial private pilot—glider certificate and for the addition of category ratings.

Practical Test Standards Description

AREAS OF OPERATION are phases of the practical test arranged in a logical sequence within each standard. They begin with Preflight Preparation and end with Postflight Procedures. The examiner, however, may conduct the practical test in any sequence that results in a complete and efficient test.

TASKS are titles of knowledge areas, flight procedures, or maneuvers appropriate to an AREA OF OPERATION.

NOTE is used to emphasize special considerations required in the AREA OF OPERATION or TASK.

REFERENCE identifies the publication(s) that describe(s) the TASK. Descriptions of TASKS are not included in the standards because this information can be found in the current issue of the listed reference. Publications other than those listed may be used for references if their content conveys substantially the same meaning as the referenced publications.

These practical test standards are based on the following references.

14 CFR part 43	Maintenance, Preventive Maintenance, Rebuilding, and Alteration
14 CFR part 61	Certification: Pilots, Flight Instructors, and Ground Instructors
14 CFR part 91	General Operating and Flight Rules
AC 00-6	Aviation Weather
AC 00-45	Aviation Weather Services
AC 61-21	Flight Training Handbook
AC 61-23	Pilot's Handbook of Aeronautical Knowledge
AC 61-65	Certification: Pilots and Flight Instructors
AC 61-84	Role of Preflight Preparation
AC 90-48	Pilots' Role in Collision Avoidance
AC 90-66	Recommended Standard Traffic Patterns and Practices for Aeronautical Operations At Airports Without Operating Control Towers.
AIM	Aeronautical Information Manual
AFD	Airport Facility Directory
NOTAM's	Notices to Airmen
Other	Soaring Flight Manual (Jeppeson Sanderson) Glider Flight Manual

The Objective lists the important elements that must be satisfactorily performed to demonstrate competency in a TASK. The Objective includes:

1. specifically what the applicant should be able to do;
2. conditions under which the TASK is to be performed; and
3. acceptable performance standards.

Use of the Practical Test Standards Book

The FAA requires that all practical tests be conducted in accordance with the appropriate practical test standards and the policies set forth in the INTRODUCTION. Applicants shall be evaluated in ALL TASKS included in each AREA OF OPERATION of the appropriate practical test standard, unless otherwise noted.

An applicant who holds a private pilot certificate seeking an additional glider category rating, will be evaluated in at least the AREAS OF OPERATION and TASKS listed in the Additional Rating Task Table located on page 9 of this practical test standard. At the discretion of the examiner, an evaluation of the applicant's competence in the remaining AREAS OF OPERATION and TASKS may be conducted.

In preparation for each practical test, the examiner shall develop a written "plan of action." The "plan of action" shall include all TASKS in each AREA OF OPERATION, unless noted otherwise. If the elements in one TASK have already been evaluated in another TASK, they need not be repeated. For example, the "plan of action" need not include evaluating the applicant on complying with markings, signals, and clearances at the end of the flight, if that element was sufficiently observed at the beginning of the flight. Any TASKS selected for evaluation during a practical test shall be evaluated in its entirety.

The examiner is not required to follow the precise order in which the AREAS OF OPERATION and TASKS appear in this book. The examiner may change the sequence or combine TASKS with similar Objectives to have an orderly and efficient flow of the practical test. For example, Boxing The Wake may be combined with Maintaining Tow Positions. The examiner's "plan of action" shall include the order and combination of TASKS to be demonstrated by the applicant in a manner that will result in an efficient and valid test.

Examiners shall place special emphasis upon those aircraft operations that are most critical to flight safety. Among these areas are precise aircraft control and sound judgment in decision making. Although these areas may or may not be shown under each TASK, they are essential to flight safety and shall receive careful evaluation throughout the practical test. If these areas are shown in the Objective, additional emphasis shall be placed on them. The examiner shall also emphasize stall/spin awareness, wake turbulence avoidance, low-level wind shear, collision avoidance, runway incursion avoidance, and checklist usage.

The examiner is expected to use good judgment in the performance of simulated emergency procedures. The use of the safest means for simulation is expected. Consideration must be given to local conditions, both meteorological and topographical, at the time of the test, as well as the applicant's workload, and the condition of the aircraft used. If the procedure being evaluated would put the maneuver in jeopardy, it is expected that the applicant will simulate that portion of the maneuver.

Practical Test Prerequisites

An applicant for the private pilot—glider practical test is required by 14 CFR part 61 to:

1. be at least 16 years of age;
2. be able to read, speak, write, and understand the English language. If there is a doubt, use AC 60-28, English Language Skill Standards;
3. hold at least a student pilot certificate;
4. have passed the appropriate private pilot knowledge test(s) since the beginning of the 24th month before the month in which he or she takes the practical test;
5. have satisfactorily accomplished the required training and obtained the aeronautical experience prescribed;

6. have an endorsement from an authorized instructor certifying that the applicant has received flight training time within 60 days preceding the date of application in preparation for the practical test, and is prepared for the practical test; and
7. also have an endorsement certifying that the applicant has demonstrated satisfactory knowledge of the subject areas in which the applicant was deficient on the airman knowledge test.

Aircraft and Equipment Required for the Practical Test

The private pilot—glider applicant is required by 14 CFR section 61.45, to provide an airworthy, certificated aircraft for use during the practical test. This section further requires that the aircraft must:

1. have fully functioning dual controls, except as provided for in 14 CFR section 61.45(c) and (e); and
2. be capable of performing all AREAS OF OPERATION appropriate to the rating sought and have no operating limitations which prohibit its use in any of the AREAS OF OPERATION required for the practical test.

Flight Instructor Responsibility

An appropriately rated flight instructor is responsible for training the private pilot applicant to acceptable standards in **all** subject matter areas, procedures, and maneuvers included in the TASKS within each AREA OF OPERATION in this practical test standard.

Because of the impact of their teaching activities in developing safe, proficient pilots, flight instructors should exhibit a high level of knowledge, skill, and the ability to impart that knowledge and skill to students.

Throughout the applicant's training, the flight instructor is responsible for emphasizing the performance of effective visual scanning and collision avoidance procedures.

Examiner[1] Responsibility

The examiner conducting the practical test is responsible for determining that the applicant meets the acceptable standards of knowledge and skill of each TASK within the appropriate practical test standard. Since there is no formal division between the "oral" and "skill" portions of the practical test, this becomes an ongoing process throughout the test. Oral questioning, to determine the applicant's knowledge of TASKS and related safety factors, should be used judiciously at all times, especially during the flight portion of the practical test.

During the flight portion of the practical test, the examiner shall evaluate the applicant's use of visual scanning and collision avoidance procedures.

Satisfactory Performance

Satisfactory performance to meet the requirements for certification is based on the applicant's ability to safely:

1. perform the TASKS specified in the AREAS OF OPERATION for the certificate or rating sought within the approved standards;
2. demonstrate mastery of the aircraft with the successful outcome of each TASK performed never seriously in doubt;
3. demonstrate satisfactory proficiency and competency within the approved standards; and
4. demonstrate sound judgment.

Unsatisfactory Performance

If, in the judgment of the examiner, the applicant does not meet the standards of performance of any TASK performed, the associated AREA OF OPERATION is failed and therefore, the practical test is failed. The examiner or applicant may discontinue the test at any time when the failure of an AREA OF OPERATION makes the applicant ineligible for the certificate or rating sought. The test may be continued ONLY with the consent of the applicant. If the test is discontinued, the applicant is entitled to credit for only those AREAS OF OPERATION and TASKS satisfactorily performed; however, during the retest, and at the discretion of the examiner, any TASK may be re-evaluated, including those previously passed.

---

[1] The word "examiner" is used throughout the standards to denote either the FAA inspector or FAA designated pilot examiner who conducts an official practical test.

Typical areas of unsatisfactory performance and grounds for disqualification are:

1. Any action or lack of action by the applicant that requires corrective intervention by the examiner to maintain safe flight.
2. Failure to use proper and effective visual scanning techniques to clear the area before and while performing maneuvers.
3. Consistently exceeding tolerances stated in the Objectives.
4. Failure to take prompt corrective action when tolerances are exceeded.

When a notice of disapproval is issued, the examiner shall record the applicant's unsatisfactory performance in terms of the AREA OF OPERATION and specific TASK failed or TASK(S) not accomplished. The AREA(S) OF OPERATION not tested and the number of practical test failures shall also be recorded.

Crew Resource Management (CRM)

CRM refers to the effective use of all available resources: human resources, hardware, and information. Human resources include all groups routinely working with the cockpit crew or pilot who are involved with decisions that are required to operate a flight safely. These groups include, but are not limited to dispatchers, cabin crewmembers, maintenance personnel, air traffic controllers, and weather services. CRM is not a single TASK, but a set of competencies that must be evident in all TASKS in this practical test standard as applied to either crew or single pilot operations.

Applicant's Use of Checklists

Throughout the practical test, the applicant is evaluated on the use of an appropriate checklist. Proper use is dependent on the specific TASK being evaluated. The situation may be such that the use of the checklist, while accomplishing elements of an Objective, would be either unsafe or impractical, especially in a single-pilot operation. In this case, a review of the checklist after the elements have been accomplished, would be appropriate. Division of attention and proper visual scanning should be considered when using a checklist.

Use of Distractions During Practical Tests

Numerous studies indicate that many accidents have occurred when the pilot has been distracted during critical phases of flight. To evaluate the applicant's ability to utilize proper control technique while dividing attention both inside and/or outside the cockpit, the examiner shall cause a realistic distraction during the flight portion of the practical test to evaluate the applicant's ability to divide attention while maintaining safe flight.

Positive Exchange of Flight Controls

During flight training, there must always be a clear understanding between students and flight instructors of who has control of the aircraft. Prior to flight, a briefing should be conducted that includes the procedure for the exchange of flight controls. A positive three-step process in the exchange of flight controls between pilots is a proven procedure and one that is strongly recommended.

When the instructor wishes the student to take control of the aircraft, he or she will say, "You have the flight controls." The student acknowledges immediately by saying, "I have the flight controls." The flight instructor again says, "You have the flight controls." When control is returned to the instructor, follow the same procedure. A visual check is recommended to verify that the exchange has occurred. There should never by any doubt as to who is flying the aircraft.

Metric Conversion Initiative

To assist pilots in understanding and using the metric measurement system, the practical test standards refer to the metric equivalent of various altitudes throughout. The inclusion of meters is intended to familiarize pilots with its use. The metric altimeter is arranged in 10 meter increments; therefore, when converting from feet to meters, the exact conversion, being too exact for practical purposes, is rounded to the nearest 10 meter increment or even altitude as necessary.

ADDITIONAL RATING TASK TABLE

ADDITION OF A GLIDER RATING TO AN EXISTING PRIVATE PILOT CERTIFICATE								
AREA OF OPER-ATION	Required TASKS are indicated by either the TASK letter(s) that apply(s) or an indication that all or none of the TASKS must be tested.							
	ASEL	ASES	AMEL	AMES	RH	RG	Balloon	Airship
I	B,C,D	B,C,D	B,C,D	B,C,D	B,C,D	B,C,D	C,D	C,D
II	A,B,C,E	A,B,C,E	A,B,C,E	A,B,C,E	A,B,C,E	A,B,C,E	ALL	A,B,C,E
III	B	B	B	B	B	B	B	B
IV	ALL*	ALL*	ALL*	ALL*	ALL*	ALL*	ALL*	ALL*
V	ALL	ALL	ALL	ALL	ALL	ALL	ALL	ALL
VI	ALL	ALL	ALL	ALL	ALL	ALL	ALL	ALL
VII	ALL	ALL	ALL	ALL	ALL	ALL	ALL	ALL
VIII	NONE	NONE	NONE	NONE	NONE	NONE	A	NONE
IX	ALL	ALL	ALL	ALL	ALL	ALL	ALL	ALL
X	ALL	ALL	ALL	ALL	ALL	ALL	ALL	ALL
XI	ALL	ALL	ALL	ALL	ALL	ALL	ALL	ALL

*EXAMINER SHALL SELECT KIND OF LAUNCH BASED ON THE APPLICANT'S QUALIFICATIONS.

LEGEND
ASEL   Airplane Single-Engine Land
ASES   Airplane Single-Engine Sea
AMEL   Airplane Multiengine Land
AMES   Airplane Multiengine Sea
RH   Rotorcraft Helicopter
RG   Rotorcraft Gyroplane

APPLICANT'S PRACTICAL TEST CHECKLIST

Private Pilot—Glider

EXAMINER'S NAME _____

LOCATION _____

DATE/TIME _____

ACCEPTABLE AIRCRAFT

- ☐ Aircraft Documents:
    Airworthiness Certificate
    Registration Certificate
    Operating Limitations
- ☐ Aircraft Maintenance Records:
    Record of Airworthiness Inspections
    Current Status of Applicable Airworthiness Directives
- € Pilot's Operating Handbook, FAA-Approved Glider Flight Manual

PERSONAL EQUIPMENT

- ☐ Practical Test Standard
- ☐ Current Aeronautical Charts
- ☐ Computer and Plotter
- ☐ Flight Plan Form
- ☐ Flight Log Form
- ☐ Current AIM, Airport Facility Directory, and Appropriate Publications

PERSONAL RECORDS

- € Identification - Photo/Signature ID
- ☐ Pilot Certificate
- ☐ Completed FAA Form 8710-1, Airman Certificate and/or Rating Application with Instructor's Signature (if applicable)
- ☐ Airman Test Report
- ☐ Pilot Logbook with Appropriate Instructor Endorsements
- ☐ FAA Form 8060-5, Notice of Disapproval (if applicable)
- ☐ Approved School Graduation Certificate (if applicable)
- ☐ Examiner's Fee (if applicable)

EXAMINER'S PRACTICAL TEST CHECKLIST

Private Pilot—Glider

APPLICANT'S NAME _____

LOCATION _____

DATE/TIME _____

I.   PREFLIGHT PREPARATION

- ☐ **A.** Certificates and Documents
- ☐ **B.** Weather Information
- ☐ **C.** Operation of Systems
- ☐ **D.** Performance and Limitations
- ☐ **E.** Aeromedical Factors

II.   PREFLIGHT PROCEDURES

- ☐ **A.** Assembly
- ☐ **B.** Ground Handling
- ☐ **C.** Preflight Inspection
- ☐ **D.** Cockpit Management
- ☐ **E.** Visual Signals

III.   AIRPORT AND GLIDERPORT OPERATIONS

- ☐ **A.** Radio Communications
- ☐ **B.** Traffic Patterns
- ☐ **C.** Airport, Runway, and Taxiway Signs, Markings, and Lighting

IV.   LAUNCHES AND LANDINGS

AERO TOW

- ☐ **A.** Before Takeoff Check
- ☐ **B.** Normal and Crosswind Takeoff
- ☐ **C.** Maintaining Tow Positions
- ☐ **D.** Slack Line
- ☐ **E.** Boxing The Wake
- ☐ **F.** Tow Release
- ☐ **G.** Abnormal Occurrences

FAA-S-8081-22

GROUND TOW (AUTO OR WINCH)

☐   **H.**   Before Takeoff Check
☐   **I.**   Normal and Crosswind Takeoff
☐   **J.**   Abnormal Occurences

SELF-LAUNCH

☐   **K.**   Engine Starting
☐   **L.**   Taxiing
☐   **M.**   Before Takeoff Check
☐   **N.**   Normal and Crosswind Takeoff and Climb
☐   **O.**   Engine Shutdown In Flight
☐   **P.**   Abnormal Occurrences

LANDINGS

☐   **Q.**   Normal and Crosswind Landing
☐   **R.**   Slips to Landing
☐   **S.**   Downwind Landing

V.   PERFORMANCE AIRSPEEDS

☐   **A.**   Minimum Sink Airspeed
☐   **B.**   Speed-To-Fly

VI.   SOARING TECHNIQUES

☐   **A.**   Thermal Soaring
☐   **B.**   Ridge and Slope Soaring
☐   **C.**   Wave Soaring

VII. PERFORMANCE MANEUVERS

☐   **A.**   Straight Glides
☐   **B.**   Turns to Headings
☐   **C.**   Steep Turns

VIII. NAVIGATION

☐   **A.**   Flight Preparation and Planning
☐   **B.**   National Airspace System

I. AREA OF OPERATION: PREFLIGHT PREPARATION

A. TASK: CERTIFICATES AND DOCUMENTS

REFERENCES: 14 CFR parts 43, 61, and 91; AC 61-23; Glider Flight Manual.

Objective. To determine that the applicant:

1. Exhibits knowledge of the elements related to certificates and documents by explaining—

   a. pilot certificate privileges and limitations.
   b. medical fitness.
   c. pilot logbook or flight records.

2. Exhibits knowledge of the elements related to certificates and documents by locating and explaining—

   a. airworthiness and registration certificates.
   b. operating limitations, placards, and instrument markings.
   c. weight and balance data and equipment list.
   d. maintenance requirements, appropriate records, airworthiness directives, and compliance records.

B. TASK: WEATHER INFORMATION

REFERENCES: AC 00-6, AC 00-45, AC 61-23, and AC 61-84; Soaring Flight Manual.

Objective. To determine that the applicant:

1. Exhibits knowledge of the elements related to weather information from various sources with emphasis on—

   a. use of weather reports, charts, and forecasts.
   b. significant weather prognostics.

2. Exhibits knowledge of the relationship of the following factors to the lifting process—

   a. pressure and temperature lapse rates.
   b. atmospheric instability.
   c. thermal index and thermal production.
   d. cloud formation and identification.
   e. frontal weather.
   f. other lifting sources.

FAA-S-8081-22

3. Explains hazards associated with flight in the vicinity of thunderstorms.
4. Makes a competent "go/no-go" decision based on available weather information.

C. TASK: OPERATION OF SYSTEMS

REFERENCES: AC 61-23; Soaring Flight Manual, Glider Flight Manual.

Objective.   To determine that the applicant:

1. Exhibits knowledge of the elements related to the operation of instruments and systems, including as appropriate—

   a. magnetic compass.
   b. yaw string or inclinometer.
   c. airspeed indicator and altimeter.
   d. variometer and total energy compensators.
   e. gyroscopic instruments.
   f. electrical.
   g. landing gear and brakes.
   h. avionics.
   i. high-lift and drag devices.
   j. oxygen equipment.

2. Correctly interprets information displayed on the instruments.

D. TASK: PERFORMANCE AND LIMITATIONS

REFERENCES: Soaring Flight Manual, Glider Flight Manual.

Objective.   To determine that the applicant:

1. Exhibits knowledge of the elements related to performance and limitations, including the use of charts, tables, data to determine performance, and the adverse effects of exceeding limitations.
2. Uses appropriate performance charts, tables, and data.
3. Computes weight and balance, and determines if the weight and center of gravity are within limits.
4. Explains the management of ballast and its effect on performance.
5. Describes the effect of various atmospheric conditions on the glider's performance.
6. Explains the applicable performance speeds and their uses.
7. Describes the relationship between airspeeds and load factors.

E. TASK: AEROMEDICAL FACTORS

REFERENCES: AIM, Soaring Flight Manual.

Objective.   To determine that the applicant exhibits knowledge of the elements related to aeromedical factors by explaining:

1. Symptoms, causes, effects, and corrective action of at least three (3) of the following—

    a. hypoxia.
    b. hyperventilation.
    c. middle ear and sinus problems.
    d. spatial disorientation.
    e. motion sickness.
    f.   carbon monoxide poisoning (self-launch).
    g. stress and fatigue.
    h. dehydration and heatstroke.

2. Effects of alcohol and drugs, including over-the-counter drugs.
3. Effects of evolved gas from scuba diving on a pilot during flight.

II. AREA OF OPERATION: PREFLIGHT PROCEDURES

A. TASK: ASSEMBLY

NOTE: If, in the judgment of the examiner, the demonstration of the glider assembly is impractical, competency may be determined by oral testing.

REFERENCES: Soaring Flight Manual, Glider Flight Manual.

Objective.   To determine that the applicant:

1. Exhibits knowledge of the elements related to assembly procedures.
2. Selects a suitable assembly area and provides sufficient crewmembers for assembly.
3. Follows an appropriate checklist.
4. Uses proper tools.
5. Handles components properly.
6. Cleans and lubricates parts, as appropriate.
7. Accounts for all tools and parts at the completion of assembly.
8. Performs post-assembly inspection, including a positive control check.

B. TASK: GROUND HANDLING

REFERENCES: Soaring Flight Manual, Glider Flight Manual.

Objective.   To determine that the applicant:

1. Exhibits knowledge of the elements related to ground handling procedures.
2. Selects the appropriate ground handling procedures and equipment for existing conditions.
3. Determines the number of crewmembers needed.
4. Handles the glider in a manner that will not result in damage during movement.
5. Secures the glider and controls, as necessary, in proper position.

C. TASK: PREFLIGHT INSPECTION

REFERENCES: Soaring Flight Manual, Glider Flight Manual.

Objective. To determine that the applicant:

1. Exhibits knowledge of the elements related to preflight inspection, including which items must be inspected, for what reasons, and how to detect possible defects.
2. Inspects the glider using the appropriate checklist.
3. Verifies the glider is in condition for safe flight, notes any discrepancies, and determines if maintenance is required.
4. Inspects the launch equipment, including towline, tow hitches, weak links, and release mechanism.

D. TASK: COCKPIT MANAGEMENT

REFERENCES: 14 CFR part 91; Glider Flight Manual.

Objective. To determine that the applicant:

1. Exhibits knowledge of the elements related to cockpit management procedures.
2. Organizes and arranges material and equipment in a manner making items readily available.
3. Briefs passengers on the use of safety belts, shoulder harnesses, and emergency procedures.
4. Utilizes all appropriate checklists.

E. TASK: VISUAL SIGNALS

REFERENCE: Soaring Flight Manual.

Objective. To determine that the applicant:

1. Exhibits knowledge of the elements related to aero tow or ground tow visual signals, as appropriate.
2. Uses, interprets, and responds to prelaunch, launch, airborne, and emergency signals, as appropriate.

III. AREA OF OPERATION: AIRPORT AND GLIDERPORT OPERATIONS

A. TASK: RADIO COMMUNICATIONS

NOTE: If radio communications are impractical, competency may be determined by oral testing.

REFERENCE: AIM.

Objective.   To determine that the applicant:

1. Exhibits knowledge of the elements related to radio communications, radio failure, and ATC light signals.
2. Selects appropriate frequencies for facilities to be used.
3. Transmits using recommended phraseology.
4. Acknowledges radio communications and complies with instructions.
5. Uses appropriate procedures for simulated radio communications failure.
6. Interprets and complies with ATC light signals.

B. TASK: TRAFFIC PATTERNS

REFERENCES: 14 CFR part 91; AC 90-66; Soaring Flight Manual.

Objective.   To determine that the applicant:

1. Exhibits knowledge of the elements related to traffic pattern procedures for gliders.
2. Follows established traffic pattern procedures.
3. Maintains awareness of other traffic in pattern.
4. Maintains proper ground track with crosswind correction, if necessary.
5. Crosses designated points at appropriate altitudes, unless conditions make such action impractical.
6. Selects touchdown and stop points.
7. Adjusts glidepath and track promptly to compensate for unexpected lift, sink, or changes in wind velocity.
8. Makes smooth, coordinated turns with a bank angle not to exceed 45° when turning final approach.
9. Adjusts flaps, spoilers, or dive brakes, as appropriate.
10. Recognizes and makes appropriate corrections for the effect of wind.
11. Completes the prescribed checklist, if applicable.

C. TASK: AIRPORT, RUNWAY, AND TAXIWAY SIGNS, MARKINGS, AND LIGHTING

REFERENCES: AC 61-23; AIM.

Objective. To determine that the applicant:

1. Exhibits knowledge of the elements related to airport, runway, and taxiway signs, markings, and lighting.
2. Identifies, interprets, and complies with appropriate airport, runway, and taxiway signs, markings, and lighting.

IV. AREA OF OPERATION: LAUNCHES AND LANDINGS

NOTE: Examiner shall select kind of launch based on the applicant's qualifications.

AERO TOW

A. TASK: BEFORE TAKEOFF CHECK

REFERENCES: Soaring Flight Manual, Glider Flight Manual.

Objective.   To determine that the applicant:

1. Exhibits knowledge of the elements related to the before takeoff check, including the reasons for checking the items, and how to detect malfunctions.
2. Establishes a course of action with crewmembers, including signals, speeds, wind, and emergency procedures.
3. Ensures that the glider is in safe operating condition.
4. Checks towline hookup and release mechanism, using the appropriate hook for the type of launch conducted.
5. Ensures no conflict with traffic prior to takeoff.
6. Completes the prescribed checklist, if applicable.

B. TASK: NORMAL AND CROSSWIND TAKEOFF

NOTE: If a crosswind condition does not exist, the applicant's knowledge of crosswind elements shall be evaluated through oral testing.

REFERENCES: Soaring Flight Manual, Glider Flight Manual.

Objective.   To determine that the applicant:

1. Exhibits knowledge of the elements related to normal and crosswind takeoff, including configurations and tow positions.
2. Uses proper signals for takeoff.
3. Lifts off at an appropriate airspeed.
4. Maintains proper position until towplane lifts off.
5. Maintains directional control and proper wind-drift correction thoughout the takeoff.
6. Maintains proper alignment with the towplane.

C. TASK: MAINTAINING TOW POSITIONS

REFERENCE: Soaring Flight Manual.

Objective. To determine that the applicant:

1. Exhibits knowledge of the elements related to high-tow (slightly above the wake) and low-tow (slightly below the wake) positions during various phases of aero tow.
2. Makes smooth and correct control applications to maintain vertical and lateral positions during high and low tow.
3. Transitions from high- to low-tow position through the wake while maintaining positive control.
4. Maintains proper tow position during turns.

D. TASK: SLACK LINE

REFERENCE: Soaring Flight Manual.

Objective. To determine that the applicant:

1. Exhibits knowledge of the elements related to the causes, hazards, and corrections related to slack line.
2. Recognizes slack line and applies immediate, positive, and smooth corrective action to eliminate slack line in various situations.

E. TASK: BOXING THE WAKE

REFERENCE: Soaring Flight Manual.

Objective. To determine that the applicant:

1. Exhibits knowledge of the elements related to boxing the wake (maneuvering around the wake).
2. Maneuvers the glider, while on tow, slightly outside the towplane's wake in a rectangular, box-like pattern.
3. Maintains proper control and coordination.

F. TASK: TOW RELEASE

REFERENCE: Soaring Flight Manual.

Objective.   To determine that the applicant:

1. Exhibits knowledge of the elements related to tow release, including related safety factors.
2. Maintains high-tow position with normal towline tension.
3. Clears the area before releasing the towline.
4. Releases the towline and confirms release by observing the towline.
5. Makes level or climbing turn.

G. TASK: ABNORMAL OCCURRENCES

REFERENCE: Soaring Flight Manual.

Objective.   To determine that the applicant:

1. Exhibits knowledge of the elements related to aero tow abnormal occurrences, for various situations, such as—

   a. towplane power loss during takeoff.
   b. towline break.
   c. towplane power failure at altitude.
   d. glider release failure.
   e. glider and towplane release failure **(oral only)**.

2. Demonstrates simulated aero tow abnormal occurrences as required by the examiner.

GROUND TOW (AUTO OR WINCH)

H. TASK: BEFORE TAKEOFF CHECK

REFERENCES: Soaring Flight Manual, Glider Flight Manual.

Objective. To determine that the applicant:

1. Exhibits knowledge of the elements related to the before takeoff check, including the reasons for checking the items, and how to detect malfunctions.
2. Establishes a course of action with crewmembers, including signals, speeds, wind direction, and emergency procedures.
3. Ensures glider is in safe operating condition.
4. Checks towline hookup and release mechanism, using the appropriate hook for the type of launch conducted.
5. Ensures no conflict with traffic prior to takeoff.
6. Completes the prescribed checklist, if applicable.

I. TASK: NORMAL AND CROSSWIND TAKEOFF

NOTE: If a crosswind condition does not exist, the applicant's knowledge of crosswind elements shall be evaluated through oral testing.

REFERENCES: Soaring Flight Manual, Glider Flight Manual.

Objective. To determine that the applicant:

1. Exhibits knowledge of the elements related to normal and crosswind takeoff, including related safety factors.
2. Uses proper signals for takeoff.
3. Maintains directional control during launch.
4. Lifts off at the proper airspeed.
5. Establishes proper initial climb pitch attitude.
6. Takes prompt action to correct high speed, low speed, or porpoising.
7. Maintains proper ground track during climb.
8. Releases in proper manner and confirms release.

FAA-S-8081-22

J. TASK: ABNORMAL OCCURRENCES

REFERENCES: Soaring Flight Manual, Glider Flight Manual.

Objective.   To determine that the applicant:

1. Exhibits knowledge of the elements related to ground tow abnormal occurrences for various situations, such as—

   a. overrunning the towline.
   b. towline break.
   c. inability to release towline.
   d. over- and under-speeding.
   e. porpoising.

2. Demonstrates simulated ground tow abnormal occurrences, as required by the examiner.

SELF-LAUNCH

K. TASK: ENGINE STARTING

REFERENCE: Glider Flight Manual.

Objective.   To determine that the applicant:

1. Exhibits knowledge of the elements related to engine starting, including various atmospheric conditions, and awareness of other persons and property during start.
2. Accomplishes recommended starting procedures.
3. Completes appropriate checklists.

L. TASK: TAXIING

REFERENCE: Glider Flight Manual.

Objective.   To determine that the applicant:

1. Exhibits knowledge of the elements related to taxiing, including the effect of wind during taxiing and appropriate control positions.
2. Performs a brake check immediately after the glider begins moving.
3. Positions flight controls properly, considering the wind.
4. Controls direction and speed without excessive use of brakes.
5. Avoids other aircraft and hazards.
6. Complies with signals.

M. TASK: BEFORE TAKEOFF CHECK

REFERENCE: Glider Flight Manual.

Objective.   To determine that the applicant:

1. Exhibits knowledge of the elements related to the before takeoff check, including the reason for checking each item and to detect malfunctions.
2. Positions the glider properly considering other aircraft, wind, and surface conditions.
3. Ensures engine temperatures and pressures are suitable for run-up and takeoff.
4. Accomplishes before takeoff checks and ensures the glider is in safe operating condition.
5. Reviews airspeeds, takeoff distance, and emergency procedures.
6. Completes appropriate checklists.

N. TASK: NORMAL AND CROSSWIND TAKEOFF AND CLIMB

NOTE: If a crosswind condition does not exist, the applicant's knowledge of crosswind elements shall be evaluated through oral testing.

REFERENCE: Glider Flight Manual.

Objective. To determine that the applicant:

1. Exhibits knowledge of the elements related to normal and crosswind takeoff and climb.
2. Positions flight controls for existing wind conditions.
3. Clears the area, taxies into takeoff position, and aligns the glider for departure.
4. Advances throttle smoothly to takeoff power.
5. Rotates at recommended airspeed, and accelerates to appropriate climb speed, +10/-5 knots.
6. Maintains takeoff power to a safe maneuvering altitude, then sets climb power.
7. Completes appropriate checklists.

O. TASK: ENGINE SHUTDOWN IN FLIGHT

REFERENCE: Glider Flight Manual.

Objective. To determine that the applicant:

1. Exhibits knowledge of the elements related to engine shutdown procedures in flight.
2. Sets power for proper engine cooling.
3. Establishes appropriate airspeed.
4. Sets electrical equipment.
5. Shuts down engine.
6. Feathers or positions propeller and stows, as applicable.
7. Selects proper static source, if applicable.
8. Completes appropriate checklists.

P. TASK: ABNORMAL OCCURRENCES

REFERENCES: Soaring Flight Manual, Glider Flight Manual.

Objective.   To determine that the applicant:

1. Exhibits knowledge of the elements related to self-launch abnormal occurrences, for various situations, such as—

    a. partial, complete power failure, and failure to gain restart.
    b. fire or smoke.
    c. electrical system malfunction.
    d. low fuel pressure.
    e. low oil pressure.
    f. engine overheat.
    g. canopy opening in flight.
    h. engine restart in flight.

2. Demonstrates simulated self-launch abnormal occurrences, as required by the examiner.

LANDINGS

Q. TASK: NORMAL AND CROSSWIND LANDING

NOTE: If a crosswind condition does not exist, the applicant's knowledge of crosswind elements shall be evaluated through oral testing.

REFERENCES: Soaring Flight Manual, Glider Flight Manual.

Objective. To determine that the applicant:

1. Exhibits knowledge of the elements related to normal and crosswind approach and landing procedures.
2. Adjusts flaps, spoilers, or dive brakes, as appropriate.
3. Maintains recommended approach airspeed, +10/-5 knots.
4. Maintains crosswind correction and directional control throughout the approach and landing.
5. Makes smooth, timely, and positive control application during the roundout and touchdown.
6. Touches down smoothly within the designated landing area, with no appreciable drift, and with the longitudinal axis aligned with the desired landing path, stopping short of and within 200 feet (120 meters) of a designated point.

> **NOTE:** The applicant shall touchdown and roll to a point designated by the examiner stopping within 200' without rolling past the designated point. The point should be far enough away from the touchdown point that it should not require more than light-medium braking to come to a stop within the required distance.

7. Maintains control during the after-landing roll.
8. Completes appropriate checklists.

R. TASK: SLIPS TO LANDING

REFERENCES: Soaring Flight Manual, Glider Flight Manual.

Objective. To determine that the applicant:

1. Exhibits knowledge of the elements related to forward, side, and turning slips to landing, with and without the use of drag devices.
2. Recognizes the situation where a slip should be used to land in a desired area.

3. Establishes a slip without the use of drag devices.
4. Maintains the desired ground track.
5. Maintains proper approach attitude.
6. Makes smooth, proper, and positive control applications during recovery from the slip.
7. Touches down smoothly within the designated landing area.

S. TASK: DOWNWIND LANDING

NOTE: This TASK may be evaluated orally at the discretion of the examiner.

REFERENCES: Soaring Flight Manual, Glider Flight Manual.

Objective.   To determine that the applicant:

1. Exhibits knowledge of the elements related to downwind landings, including safety related factors.
2. Adjusts flaps, spoilers, or dive brakes, as appropriate.
3. Maintains recommended approach airspeed, ±5 knots.
4. Uses proper downwind landing procedures.
5. Maintains proper directional control during touchdown and roll-out.
6. Applies brake smoothly to bring glider to a stop.

V. AREA OF OPERATION: PERFORMANCE AIRSPEEDS

A. TASK: MINIMUM SINK AIRSPEED

REFERENCES: Soaring Flight Manual, Glider Flight Manual.

Objective.   To determine that the applicant:

1. Exhibits knowledge of the elements related to aerodynamic factors and use of minimum sink airspeed.
2. Determines the minimum sink airspeed for a given situation and maintains the selected speed, ±5 knots.

B. TASK: SPEED-TO-FLY

REFERENCES: Soaring Flight Manual, Glider Flight Manual.

Objective.   To determine that the applicant:

1. Exhibits knowledge of the elements related to speed-to-fly, and its uses.
2. Determines the speed-to-fly for a given situation and maintains the speed, ±5 knots.

VI. AREA OF OPERATION: SOARING TECHNIQUES

NOTE: Due to varying geographical locations and atmospheric conditions, the applicant may be asked to demonstrate at least one of the following soaring TASKS most appropriate for the particular location and existing conditions.

If conditions do not permit a demonstration of soaring skills, applicants will be expected to demonstrate knowledge of the various types of soaring through oral testing.

A. TASK: THERMAL SOARING

REFERENCE: Soaring Flight Manual.

Objective.   To determine that the applicant:

1. Exhibits knowledge of the elements related to thermal soaring.
2. Recognizes the indications of, and the presence of, a thermal.
3. Analyzes the thermal structure and determines the direction to turn to remain within the thermal.
4. Exhibits coordinated control and planning when entering and maneuvering to remain within the thermal.
5. Applies correct techniques to re-enter the thermal, if lift is lost.
6. Remains oriented to ground references, wind, and other aircraft.
7. Maintains proper airspeeds in and between thermals.

B. TASK: RIDGE AND SLOPE SOARING

REFERENCE: Soaring Flight Manual.

Objective.   To determine that the applicant:

1. Exhibits knowledge of the elements related to ridge and slope soaring.
2. Recognizes terrain features and wind conditions which create orographic lift.
3. Enters the area of lift properly.
4. Estimates height and maintains a safe distance from the terrain.
5. Exhibits smooth, coordinated control, and planning to remain within the area of lift.
6. Uses correct technique to re-enter the area of lift, if lift is lost.

7. Remains oriented to ground references, wind, and other aircraft.
8. Uses proper procedures and techniques when crossing ridges.
9. Maintains proper airspeeds.

C. TASK: WAVE SOARING

REFERENCE: Soaring Flight Manual.

Objective.   To determine that the applicant:

1. Exhibits knowledge of the elements related to wave soaring.
2. Locates and enters the area of lift.
3. Exhibits smooth, coordinated control, and planning to remain within the area of lift.
4. Uses correct technique to re-enter the area of lift, if lift is lost.
5. Remains oriented to ground references, wind, and other aircraft.
6. Recognizes and avoids areas of possible extreme turbulence.
7. Maintains proper airspeeds.
8. Coordinates with ATC, as appropriate.

VII. AREA OF OPERATION: PERFORMANCE MANEUVERS

A. TASK: STRAIGHT GLIDES

REFERENCE: Soaring Flight Manual.

Objective.   To determine that the applicant:

1. Exhibits knowledge of the elements related to straight glides, including the relationship of pitch attitude and airspeed.
2. Tracks toward a prominent landmark at a specified airspeed.
3. Demonstrates the effect of flaps, spoilers, or dive brakes, if equipped, in relation to pitch attitude and airspeed.
4. Exhibits smooth, coordinated control, and planning.
5. Maintains the specified heading, $\pm10°$, and the specified airspeed, ±10 knots.

B. TASK: TURNS TO HEADINGS

REFERENCE: Soaring Flight Manual.

Objective.   To determine that the applicant:

1. Exhibits knowledge of the elements related to turns to headings, including the relationship of pitch attitude, bank angle, and airspeed.
2. Enters and maintains an appropriate rate of turn with smooth, proper, and coordinated control applications.
3. Maintains the desired airspeed, ±10 knots, and rolls out on the specified heading, $\pm10°$.

C. TASK: STEEP TURNS

REFERENCES: Soaring Flight Manual, Glider Flight Manual.

Objective.   To determine that the applicant:

1. Exhibits knowledge of the elements related to steep turns, including load factor, effect on stall speed, and overbanking tendency.
2. Establishes the recommended entry airspeed.
3. Enters a turn maintaining a bank angle of $45°/\pm5°$, with smooth and coordinated control applications.
4. Maintains desired airspeed, ±10 knots.
5. Recovers with smooth and coordinated control application within 10° of the desired heading.

VIII. AREA OF OPERATION: NAVIGATION

NOTE: The applicant's knowledge of this AREA OF OPERATION will be evaluated through oral testing.

A. TASK: FLIGHT PREPARATION AND PLANNING

REFERENCES: AC 61-23; AIM, Soaring Flight Manual.

Objective.   To determine that the applicant:

1. Exhibits knowledge of the elements related to flight preparations and planning.
2. Selects and uses current and appropriate aeronautical charts.
3. Plots a course and selects prominent en route checkpoints.
4. Constructs a flight profile to determine minimum flight altitude at go-ahead points.
5. Explains method of using lift sources and speeds effectively within and between lift sources.
6. Selects available landing area.
7. Describes coordination procedures with air traffic control, as appropriate.

B. TASK: NATIONAL AIRSPACE SYSTEM

REFERENCES: 14 CFR part 91; AIM.

Objective.   To determine that the applicant exhibits knowledge of the elements related to the National Airspace System by explaining:

1. Basic VFR weather minimums for all classes of airspace.
2. Airspace classes and their dimensions, pilot certification, and glider equipment requirements for the following—

   a. Class A.
   b. Class B.
   c. Class C.
   d. Class D.
   e. Class E.
   f. Class G.

3. Special use airspace and other airspace areas.

IX. AREA OF OPERATION: SLOW FLIGHT AND STALLS

A. TASK: MANEUVERING AT MINIMUM CONTROL AIRSPEED

REFERENCES: Soaring Flight Manual, Glider Flight Manual.

Objective.   To determine that the applicant:

1. Exhibits knowledge of the elements related to maneuvering at minimum control airspeed, including flight characteristics and controllability.
2. Establishes and maintains the airspeed at which any further increase in angle of attack or change in configurations would result in a stall in straight or turning flight in various configurations and bank angles.
3. Adjusts the airspeed to avoid stalls in turbulent air or as bank is increased.
4. Applies control inputs in a smooth and coordinated manner.
5. Uses proper procedures to avoid stalls when raising a lowered wing.
6. Maintains heading, ±10°, during straight flight, and the desired bank angle, ±10°, during turns.

B. TASK: STALL RECOGNITION AND RECOVERY

REFERENCES: Soaring Flight Manual, Glider Flight Manual.

Objective.   To determine that the applicant:

1. Exhibits knowledge of the elements related to stall recognition and recovery, including the aerodynamic factors and flight situations that may result in stalls, and the hazards of stalling during uncoordinated flight.
2. Selects an entry altitude that will allow the maneuver to be completed no lower than 1,500 feet AGL.
3. Establishes and maintains a pitch attitude that will result in a stall during both straight and turning flight with and without flaps, spoilers, or dive brakes, as appropriate.
4. Maintains a specified bank angle of up to 15° of bank, ±10°, during turns.
5. Recovers at the stall.
6. Uses smooth and coordinated control applications throughout the maneuver.

X. AREA OF OPERATION: EMERGENCY OPERATIONS

NOTE: These TASKS are knowledge only.

A. TASK: SIMULATED OFF-AIRPORT LANDING

REFERENCES: Soaring Flight Manual, Glider Flight Manual.

Objective.   To determine that the applicant exhibits knowledge of the elements related to a simulated off-airport landing, including selection of a suitable landing area and the procedures used to accomplish an off-airport landing.

B. TASK: EMERGENCY EQUIPMENT AND SURVIVAL GEAR

REFERENCES: Soaring Flight Manual, Glider Flight Manual.

Objective.   To determine that the applicant exhibits knowledge of the elements related to emergency equipment and survival gear, appropriate to the glider used for the practical test, by describing:

1. Location in the glider.
2. Method of operation or use.
3. Servicing and storage.
4. Inspection, fitting, and use of parachutes.
5. Equipment and gear appropriate for operation in various climates and over various types of terrain.

XI. AREA OF OPERATION: POSTFLIGHT PROCEDURES

TASK: AFTER-LANDING AND SECURING

REFERENCES: Soaring Flight Manual, Glider Flight Manual.

Objective. To determine that the applicant:

1. Exhibits knowledge of the elements related to after-landing and securing procedures, including local and ATC operations, ramp safety, parking hand signals, shutdown (if appropriate), securing, and postflight inspection.
2. Selects a suitable parking area while considering wind and safety of nearby persons and property.
3. Taxies to parking area and performs engine shutdown, if applicable.
4. Services the glider, if applicable.
5. Secures the glider properly.
6. Performs a satisfactory postflight inspection.
7. Completes the prescribed checklist.

www.ingramcontent.com/pod-product-compliance
Lightning Source LLC
Chambersburg PA
CBHW060629030426
42337CB00018B/3277